The Art of Wealth Making

ESCAPING THE MIDDLE-CLASS TRAP

REHAN JAIN

Table of Contents

Introduction: The Great Middle-Class Illusion 1

1. The "Log Kya Kahenge" Tax 7

2. The "YOLO" and "FOMO" Virus 15

3. The Digital Illusion 25

4. The Hedonic Treadmill 33

5. The Toxic Myth: "Saving Se Ameer Nahi Bante" 41

6. The EMI Millionaires 49

7. The "21 Din Mein Paisa Double" Trap 59

8. The Middle-Class Guilt 67

9. The "Safe" Investment Illusion 77

10. Eenth Aur Sona 87

11. The Wedding Bankruptcy 97

12. "Mera Beta Hi Mera Retirement Plan Hai" 105

13. Mehngai: The Silent Thief 113

14. From Earner to Owner 121

A Final Note of Gratitude: The Journey Ahead 129

COPYRIGHT & DISCLAIMER

⚠ **Important Regulatory and Legal Disclaimer**

Educational Content Only: This book is an educational blueprint structured strictly for financial literacy and behavioral analysis. Nothing within these pages constitutes an explicit or implicit recommendation, solicitation, advisory, or endorsement to buy, sell, or hold any specific financial instrument or asset class. Securities markets carry inherent structural risks; past records do not guarantee future outcomes.

No Advisory Architecture: The author is not a SEBI Registered Investment Advisor (RIA), licensed stockbroker, or certified financial planner. Consuming this content does not establish an advisor-client relationship. Every individual's financial matrix is unique; you are directed to conduct your own forensic analysis and consult a certified financial expert before deploying real capital.

Absolute Ownership: The exact millisecond you take action based on the concepts learned in this book, you assume 100% legal, financial, and moral liability for all resulting gains or losses. Owning your choices completely is the absolute first rule of a rich mindset.

"Seek wealth, not money or status. Wealth is having assets that earn while you sleep. Status is your place in the social hierarchy."

— Naval Ravikant

"Too many people spend money they haven't earned, to buy things they don't want, to impress people that they don't like."

— Will Rogers

Introduction: The Great Middle-Class Illusion

There is a silent, devastating tragedy unfolding in millions of households today. It is the ultimate paradox of our generation, and it is the absolute hardest truth you will ever have to accept: **In a desperate, exhausting attempt to *look* like the upper class, the average middle-class earner is mathematically pushing themselves down into the lower class.**

We live in an era of rented status. We buy cars we cannot afford to impress people we do not even like. We finance flagship smartphones on 24-month EMIs just to maintain a social aesthetic. We blow up a decade of savings on three-day destination weddings just to win a fleeting applause from society. On the outside, our Instagram feeds and social gatherings project the ultimate illusion of wealth and arrival. But behind closed doors, behind the forced smiles and the designer clothes, there is a suffocating, terrifying anxiety.

The truth is, you are not moving forward. You are sprinting on an invisible treadmill, burning all your energy and capital just to ensure you don't fall off.

You are not failing financially because you do not work hard enough. You are failing because you are playing a game with rigged rules, using a script handed to you by a society that benefits from your financial ignorance. You have been conditioned since childhood to equate a high salary with wealth, to view heavy debt as "normal," and to treat your children as your retirement policies.

This book is not a gentle, feel-good financial guide. This is a brutal, necessary intervention.

Before we can build your wealth, we must stop your bleeding. Over the next 14 chapters, we are going to surgically remove the

"Financial Cancer" that is eating away at your future. We are going to tear down the generational myths, expose the toxic show-off culture, decode the silent thief of inflation, and dismantle the emotional traps that have kept your family financially paralyzed for decades.

You are about to unlearn everything you thought you knew about money. It will be uncomfortable, it will hit close to home, and it will challenge your deepest beliefs. But by the time you reach the final page, you will be completely financially awake. You will no longer be a pawn in the system; you will be ready to own the machine.

Welcome to *The Art of Wealth Making*. It is time to step off the treadmill. It is time to escape the trap.

“The greatest fear in the world is of the opinions of others. And the moment you are unafraid of the crowd you are no longer a sheep, you become a lion."

— Osho

"Spending money to show people how much money you have is the fastest way to have less money."

— Morgan Housel

1.

The "Log Kya Kahenge" Tax

The invisible price of pleasing society

In India, the greatest destroyer of wealth is not stock market crashes, bad investments, or even inflation. The greatest destroyer of wealth is a simple, four-word question we have been programmed to ask since childhood:

"Log kya kahenge?" (What will people say?)

Think about it. This invisible fear dictates almost every major decision in a middle-class Indian's life. It decides which stream we choose in high school (science, of course), which degree we pursue, what kind of trips we should take, which car to run, and how grand our weddings should be. But as we grow older and start earning our own money, this childhood conditioning silently leaks into our bank accounts.

Without even realizing it, we start spending our hard-earned money to buy things we don't need, to impress people we don't even like—or even worse, the people we don't even know (social media followers).

The Invisible Audience in Your Wallet

Every time you make a major purchase, there is an invisible audience standing right behind you. This audience consists of your extended relatives, your neighbors, your college friends, and your Instagram followers.

Have you ever noticed how, right before the festival of Diwali, families suddenly rush to buy a larger television or upgrade their sofa set? They don't do it because the old TV stopped working, or the sofa set has worn down or become uncomfortable. They do it because guests are coming over, and the old TV or the old sofa set "looks a bit cheap." Or, consider a young professional who upgrades to the newest iPhone on EMI (thanks to Buy Now Pay Later), simply because pulling out a two-year-old Android phone in a corporate meeting feels embarrassing.

Let me tell you a real story about a friend of mine—Kartik Gupta, a 37-year-old Senior Data Analyst living in Delhi.

For years, Kartik had a strict personal ritual: every two years, he would buy the absolute top model of the newly launched iPhone. He wouldn't just buy it; he would pre-order it within the first 48 to 72 hours of its global launch. It became his signature. In his entire social circle, he was known as "The Guy with the latest iPhone."

The reality? His older phone was always in perfect condition. A premium phone easily runs without a single glitch for three to five years. Yet, Kartik was paying a massive amount every second year, not for a better camera or a faster processor, but simply to feed his status.

But eventually, the trap closed in on him. One year, he decided to finally break the ritual and skip the upgrade. His current phone was working flawlessly, and he wanted to save that money. But society had other plans. When his friends and colleagues noticed he was carrying the older model, the whispers started.

Soon, people were actually walking up to him, asking with fake sympathy, "Brother, is everything okay? Why didn't you buy the new iPhone this time? Are you facing some financial problems?"

Can you imagine that suffocating anxiety? Kartik wasn't broke, but society made him feel like a complete failure just because he chose not to waste money. The pressure became so heavy, the fear of *Log kya kahenge* so unbearable, that just a few weeks later, he quietly went and bought the latest iPhone. He even had to invent a fake story, lying to everyone that his initial pre-order had simply gotten delayed.

He didn't buy that phone for himself. He bought it to escape the judgment of the invisible audience. When you make decisions like this, you are no longer buying a product for its utility. You are paying a premium for social validation. What you are actually paying is the Status Tax.

Defining The "Status Tax"

What exactly is the Status Tax? Let's look at some simple math.

A ₹25,000 smartphone does exactly what a phone is supposed to do. It makes calls, takes decent pictures, runs WhatsApp and Instagram, runs YouTube, and gives you access to the internet. A ₹1,50,000 phone does the exact same things, but it comes with a shiny logo of a half-eaten apple on the back.

The ₹1,25,000 difference between the two phones is not the cost of technology. That ₹1,25,000 is the Status Tax. It is the fee you pay to society to signal that "you are successful".

This obsession with spending money just to flaunt social status is not a modern invention. Way back in 1899, a brilliant economist named Thorstein Veblen noticed this exact human flaw and coined the term "Conspicuous Consumption." His research proved that individuals often purchase luxury goods not for their actual utility, but as a public display of economic power and social standing.

More than a century later, the modern Indian middle class is still falling face-first into this *sadiyon purani* psychological weakness. The tragic part of the Indian middle-class story is that we are paying the highest Status Tax in the world, and we are doing it using money we haven't even earned yet. Thanks to Credit Cards and "No-Cost EMIs," young Indians are trading years of their future freedom just to look rich today.

The "Man in the Car" Paradox

Now, imagine you buying a shiny ₹25 Lakh SUV on a massive 7-year car loan. You drive it out of the showroom, roll down the windows, and stop at a traffic light. You notice people looking at you. You feel a rush of pride. Right! You think, "Yes! They are looking at me. They are respecting me because I have proved to them that I am successful."

But are you aware of the harsh reality? Nobody—nobody—is looking at you.

People are looking at the car. And in their heads, they are imagining *themselves* driving it. They don't care about who is the driver.

This profound psychological insight was famously highlighted by renowned financial writer Morgan Housel in his global bestseller, *The Psychology of Money*. He termed this phenomenon the "Man in the Car Paradox." The paradox is simple yet brutal: you mistakenly believe that people will admire and respect you if you drive an expensive car, but in reality, they completely bypass you because they are too busy using your asset as a prop for their own daydreams.

Because of this illusion, you took on a massive debt, sacrificed a huge chunk of your monthly salary, and locked yourself into a stressful corporate job for the next seven years. You wanted respect and admiration, but the expensive car failed to buy either. It only bought you a monthly EMI message from your bank.

True Wealth is Silent

We need to understand the fundamental difference between *looking rich* and *being wealthy*.

Looking rich is loud. It is the branded clothes, the expensive car, the mirror-selfie showcasing the branded phone, and the luxury vacations posted on social media. But very often, the people who look the richest have the highest amount of debt (Loans-EMIs). Their entire paycheck disappears within two weeks of every month just to maintain the illusion of their Richie Rich lifestyle.

Being wealthy, on the other hand, is silent. Wealth is the money you *did not* spend. Wealth is the ₹1,25,000 you saved by not buying the expensive phone and instead putting it into a Mutual Fund or FD. Wealth is the peace of mind you feel when you go to sleep, knowing you have zero EMIs. Wealth is having enough money saved up so that if your boss shouts at you tomorrow, you can confidently walk away without worrying about how you will pay next month's rent.

True Wealth gives you control over the most expensive and non-recoverable thing in the world—"your time".

True financial freedom begins the exact moment you decide to fire your invisible audience. Society will happily and loudly applaud your expensive lifestyle, but they will not come to pay your bills when you go broke.

Stop going broke trying to look rich

Summary

- **The Invisible Audience:** You are heavily conditioned to spend money based on what society thinks, not what you actually need.
- **The Status Tax:** The extra money you pay just for a brand name or a shiny logo is a tax on your future wealth.
- **Wealth is Silent:** Looking rich requires spending money, being wealthy requires saving and investing it. Respect comes from your character, not from your car or expensive vacations.

Action Step: The Status Audit

Take out a pen and paper or open a note on your phone. Look at your major expenses over the last 6 months. Be brutally honest with yourself. Which of these did you buy for actual utility, and which ones did you buy to pay the "Status Tax"?

Add up the total amount of your Status Tax and fill the amount in the below table. After every 6 months, I would ask you to come back here, re-do the calculation and fill the amount in the table, to find out how much you have improved and successfully been able to remove/reduce your status tax.

Fill in the amount of your Status Tax in the table below:

Date	Status Tax
Last 6 Months	

"Chaah gayi, chinta miti, manwa beparwah;
Jisko kuch nahi chahiye, wahi shahenshah."
(When desires vanish and worries fade, the mind becomes carefree. He who needs nothing to prove his worth, is the true emperor.)

— Kabir Das

"Comparison is the thief of joy."

— Theodore Roosevelt

2.
The "YOLO" and "FOMO" Virus

How social media engineers your bankruptcy

There is a universal cycle that almost every young working professional in India goes through every single week. It is called the "Weekend Illusion."

It starts on Friday evening. At 6:00 PM, a sudden wave of excitement hits you. You feel you have worked hard all week and you *deserve* to treat yourself. But by Monday morning, as you stand in the crowded metro or sit in traffic, a deep dread washes over you. You open your banking app, look at your drained account balance, and silently ask yourself, *"Where did all my money go?"*

The answer lies in two toxic viruses that have infected our generation: YOLO and FOMO.

"You Only Live Once" (YOLO) was originally a beautiful philosophy. It meant you should take risks, pursue your passions, and live life to the fullest. But today, modern social media has hijacked this phrase—YOLO has simply become a toxic excuse for poor financial discipline.

The "Weekend Warrior" Trap

Meet Kabir, a software engineer living in Delhi-NCR, the ultimate "Weekend Warrior."

Kabir's weekends are fully booked. He constantly reloads his digital wallets to buy overpriced lattes at premium cafes, chasing that coveted "Gold Tier" customer status. He orders fancy, expensive crispy burgers just to click the perfect aesthetic picture for his Instagram stories. When a popular international artist announces a concert, Kabir buys the VIP tickets—not because he even listens to that artist, but simply because *"everyone else is going."* Kabir suffers from a severe case of FOMO: Fear Of Missing Out.

While it feels like a casual piece of internet slang, the word FOMO actually has a deeply researched academic origin. In 2004, a Harvard Business School student named Patrick J. McGinnis officially coined the term in an academic paper to describe the psychological anxiety of missing out on shared social experiences. Modern social media algorithms have simply taken this underlying mental vulnerability and turned it into a full-blown financial epidemic for our generation.

For people like Kabir, staying home on a Saturday night feels like a social crime. There is a constant, suffocating anxiety of watching others' stories, seeing them at fancy clubs or taking weekend trips to a hill station, and feeling an overwhelming urge to immediately go out and spend. They swipe their credit cards simply to scream to the digital world, *"Hey, look at me! I exist, and I am having a great time too!"*

But there is an antidote to this exhausting lifestyle, and it is called **POMO**—the Pleasure Of Missing Out (also known as JOMO, the Joy Of Missing Out).

POMO is the ultimate financial superpower. It is the quiet confidence of realizing that you don't have to attend every party, eat at every new cafe, or buy every trending gadget. It is the profound peace of staying home, reading a book, and watching your wealth grow while the rest of the world goes broke trying to impress and seek respect and admiration from others.

Let's look at how the FOMO mindset destroys wealth, while the POMO mindset quietly builds it:

POMO vs FOMO: The Financial Impact

Feature	FOMO Mindset (Wealth Destroyer)	POMO Mindset (Wealth Creator)
Investing Style	"Everyone is buying this, I should too!" (Buying High)	"I don't understand this hype; I will stay away." (Capital Protection)
Spending Habit	Showing off using Credit Cards and EMIs (Debt Trap).	Spending based on actual needs and maintaining a high savings rate.
Mental Peace	Checking portfolios and social status every hour (High Anxiety).	Putting money in Index Funds or FDs and sleeping peacefully.

The True Cost of "Living in the Moment"

You might think, *"It's just one weekend, what is the big deal?"* Let's look at the harsh reality of small, recurring expenses.

Let's assume this FOMO lifestyle costs you just ₹4,000 every weekend. Between cafes, movies, fast food, and cab rides, this is a very conservative estimate—that equals roughly ₹16,000 a month. Over a single year, that is roughly ₹2 Lakhs, all spent on temporary thrills and aesthetic pictures that disappear in 24 hours.

Now, let's look at the "Cost of FOMO."

If you embraced POMO, stayed home a few weekends, and quietly invested that same ₹16,000 every month in an index fund giving a historical return of roughly 12% CAGR, do you know what that money would become? In 10 years, that weekend cafe money would turn into a massive corpus of roughly **₹36 Lakhs**. And in 20 years, roughly **₹1.5 Crores**.

That is what you are giving up. You are trading Lakhs and Crores of future freedom for a few overpriced burgers and social media likes today.

To permanently cure yourself of this weekend spending cycle, you must practice the golden rule of the world's greatest investor, Warren Buffett. He famously advised, **"Do not save what is left after spending, but spend what is left after saving."** When you choose the POMO mindset, you don't wait for Monday morning to see what is left in your account. You automate your wealth machine on the 1st of the month through a SIP, and then guilt-free spend whatever remains.

From YOLO to YODO

We need a massive mindset shift. "Fake it till you make it" is the absolute worst financial advice ever given to our generation.

It is time to replace YOLO with YODO: **You Only Die Once. You Live Every Day.**

Real YOLO isn't about blowing your entire paycheck on a Sunday brunch just to look cool. It is not about booking a foreign trip just to prove that you "belong" to the elite travel club, maxing out your credit cards to post luxury pictures online—while secretly hunting for the cheapest, most uncomfortable options off-camera. Taking a vacation to impress others, only to come back and spend the next six months suffocating under credit card bills and EMI stress, is not living life to the fullest. It is financial slavery.

Real YOLO is having enough financial backing to take a 6-month break to travel the world peacefully, without taking any loans. Real YOLO is the ultimate freedom to walk into a toxic boss's cabin and quit your job without panicking about next month's rent.

Having fun is important, but your fun today should never come at the cost of your freedom tomorrow.

Summary

- **The Weekend Illusion:** Using YOLO as an excuse for reckless spending is keeping the modern working professional trapped in a paycheck-to-paycheck cycle.
- **FOMO vs POMO:** The Fear of Missing Out creates anxiety and debt. The Pleasure of Missing Out creates peace of mind and massive wealth.
- **The True Cost:** Small weekend expenses compound over time. You are trading lakhs and crores of rupees in future wealth for temporary digital validation today.

Action Step: The Weekend Audit

Open your UPI app or bank statement right now. Look at your transaction history for the last 12 weekends. Isolate the money you spent *only* because of boredom, peer pressure, or the urge to post on social media. Write the total amount in the table below, and repeat the same exercise after 12 weeks to track your progress.

Date	Validation Cost
Last 12 Weekends	

"In the digital world, convenience is a tax you pay on your wealth. The easier it is to spend money, the harder it is to become rich."

— Kunal Shah

"Beware of little expenses; a small leak will sink a great ship."

— Benjamin Franklin

3.
The Digital Illusion

How technology secretly hacks your wallet

Think back to the time when we primarily used cash. Imagine you are standing at a store, buying a pair of shoes. You open your wallet, pull out five crisp ₹500 notes, and hand them over to the cashier. As those notes leave your hand, your brain registers a tiny pinch of psychological discomfort.

This isn't just a feeling; it is a scientifically proven phenomenon. In 1996, behavioral economists *Dan Ariely* and *Ofer Zellermayer* conducted extensive research on human spending habits and coined a brilliant term for this: **The "Pain of Paying."** Their research proved that when we physically hand over cash, the pain centers in our brain literally light up. This pain was a natural defense mechanism—it forced you to pause and subconsciously ask, *"Is this purchase really worth my hard-earned money?"*

Today, technology has completely assassinated that pain. With a 4-digit PIN, a fingerprint tap, or a quick Face ID scan, your money disappears into the digital void. We are so worried about the physical radiation and waves emitted by our phones when we hold them close to our brains, fearing long-term health issues. Yet, we completely ignore the invisible "algorithmic waves" that are continuously and silently draining our bank accounts.

Frictionless payments are marketed to us as a grand convenience, but in reality, they are the ultimate wealth destroyers.

Death by a Thousand Cuts

Meet Aman. If you ask Aman about his financial habits, he will proudly tell you that he is very frugal. He doesn't buy luxury cars, he doesn't wear expensive watches, and he rarely goes on international vacations. Yet, at the end of every month, his bank account is completely empty.

Aman's wealth is not being destroyed by one massive purchase—it is bleeding out through a thousand tiny cuts.

His day starts with a quick digital reload of ₹351 on his favorite coffee app—partially because he needs the caffeine, but mostly to maintain his digital "Gold" membership status. During his lunch break, he scrolls through Instagram. The algorithm, which tracks his searches and knows his deepest insecurities, shows him a highly targeted ad for a new grooming gadget with a flashing "Limited Time Offer!" tag. Without a second thought, he hits 'Buy Now' with a single tap.

Late at night, he gets a craving and opens a food delivery app like Swiggy. He selects a snack worth ₹150. But the app shows a ₹40 delivery fee. To "save" himself from paying that delivery fee, Aman adds another item to cross the ₹220 free-delivery threshold.

His total bill is now ₹250. He proudly thinks he hacked the system—completely ignoring the fact that he just spent ₹100 extra to save a ₹40 fee. Aman thinks, *"It is just ₹100 or ₹200—what difference does it make?"* He doesn't realize that the algorithms and UPI apps are playing him like a puppet.

The ₹150 Leakage

Let us look at the compounding disaster of small, untracked digital payments.

If you mindlessly tap your UPI app just twice a day for ₹150 each—maybe for a quick cab upgrade, a late-night dessert, or a premium app subscription—that is ₹300 a day. That translates to ₹9,000 every single month.

Now, add just one algorithmic impulse buy (like that grooming gadget or a fast-fashion jacket) worth ₹3,000 in that month. Your total invisible leakage is ₹12,000 a month. Over a year, that is roughly **₹1.44 Lakhs** wiped out from your net worth.

And the worst part? You have absolutely no major assets to show for it. It just vanished into the digital air.

Build Your Own Friction

We need a major mindset shift regarding our devices. You have to realize that "saved credit cards," "one-click checkouts," and "Face ID payments" were not invented for your convenience. They were engineered for the tech companies' profits. The easier it is to pay, the faster you will spend.

If you want to protect your wealth, you have to manually re-introduce the "Pain of Paying." You have to build your own friction.

Turn off personalized ads in your phone settings so the algorithm stops feeding on your desires. If you want to buy something online, make it a strict rule that you will not use a saved card. Force yourself to get up, find your wallet, pull out your physical debit or credit card, and manually type in that 16-digit number, the expiry date, and the CVV.

That two-minute friction gives your brain the exact amount of time it needs to wake up and ask, *"Do I really need this, or am I just bored?"*

Summary

- **The Missing Pain:** Technology has removed the psychological "Pain of Paying," making it dangerously easy to part with your money without thinking.
- **The Digital Puppet:** Algorithms know your weaknesses better than you do, and features like "free delivery thresholds" are designed to make you overspend.
- **The Leakage:** Small, frictionless UPI taps act like a leaking bucket, silently destroying lakhs of rupees of potential wealth every year.

Action Step: The Digital Detox Audit

Pick up your phone right now. Open your top 3 shopping and food delivery apps, go to the payment settings, and **delete all your saved credit and debit cards**. Make it intentionally difficult to spend money.

Next, remove the UPI app from your phone's home screen. Hide it deep inside a folder on the second or third page, so it takes at least 3 extra, intentional clicks to reach it. Re-introduce friction, and watch your savings grow.

"Desire is never satisfied by the enjoyment of desires; it only grows stronger and burns fiercer, just like a fire fed with ghee."

— The Mahabharata

"It is not the man who has too little, but the man who craves more, that is poor."

— Seneca

4.

The Hedonic Treadmill

Salary double, kharcha triple: The lifestyle creep trap

We have all said this exact line at least once in our lives: *"Man, if my salary just hits ₹1 Lakh a month, my life will be set."*

And then, miraculously, through hard work and promotions, you finally hit that ₹1 Lakh mark. For the first two months, it feels amazing. But by the third month, you look at your bank account on the 25th and realize you are still broke.

Instantly, the goalpost shifts. A new voice in your head says, *"Ah, if my salary just reaches ₹2 Lakhs, then my life is definitely set."* This story repeats after every single appraisal.

This is not a math problem; it is a psychological trap known as the **"Hedonic Treadmill"** (or Hedonic Adaptation). Imagine running on a literal gym treadmill. No matter how fast you run, you stay in the exact same spot. Financially, as your income increases, your desires and expectations increase at the exact same speed—keeping your actual wealth at absolute zero.

In 1955, British naval historian *C. Northcote Parkinson* coined an adage that perfectly defines this middle-class tragedy. It is known as **Parkinson's Law**, and it states: *"Expenses expand to match the income available."*

The "Upgrade" Trap

Let's look at how this trap plays out in the real world. Meet Harsh.

Harsh just got a massive promotion, and his salary jumped from ₹70,000 to ₹1,40,000 a month. Before this promotion, he was perfectly happy taking the metro to work and living in a modest, shared flat with a roommate.

But now, Harsh has a "Manager" title. And his mind tells him that a Manager cannot be seen taking the metro or living like a college student.

So, the upgrades begin. He moves out of the shared flat and rents a premium 2BHK, instantly doubling his rent. To solve the commute problem, he takes out a massive 7-year car loan and buys a shiny, ₹25 Lakh Korean SUV. He cancels his neighborhood gym membership and joins a premium wellness club.

His salary doubled, but his EMIs and fixed expenses tripled. Today, Harsh is making more money than he ever has in his life, but he is financially more stressed, anxious, and broke than he was during his intern days.

The 100% Lifestyle Inflation

Let's break down the math to see how a massive promotion actually made Harsh poorer.

Harsh received a ₹70,000 monthly raise. Here is where the new money went:

- **Upgraded Rent:** ₹15,000
- **New Car EMI:** ₹30,000
- **Premium Gym & Weekend Upgrades:** ₹15,000
- **Increased Taxes:** ₹10,000
- **Net Savings from the Raise:** ₹0

What is the true cost of this immediate gratification? Let's look at the opportunity cost.

What if Harsh had practiced delayed gratification? What if he allowed himself to upgrade his lifestyle by ₹35,000, but quietly invested the remaining ₹35,000 from his raise into a simple SIP?

If he had done that, in 10 years, that single promotion would have built a massive corpus of roughly **₹80 Lakhs**. By trying to immediately *look* like a manager to society, Harsh paid an invisible tax of ₹80 Lakhs.

The 50% Rule

Earning more is a fantastic thing, and you absolutely *should* enjoy the fruits of your hard work. The goal of financial freedom is not to live like a miserable monk forever. The goal is **controlled upgrades**.

To escape the Hedonic Treadmill, you need to introduce the golden **"50% Rule" (Save the Raise).**

The rule is brilliantly simple: Every time you get a salary hike, an annual bonus, or an unexpected profit, commit to automatically investing exactly 50% of that *new* money. You are completely free to upgrade your lifestyle, buy nicer clothes, or eat at better places with the remaining 50%.

This guarantees that as your standard of living goes up, your wealth machine scales up right alongside it. If saving 50% of your raise feels impossible right now, do not panic. Start with 25% or even 20%. The exact number matters less than building the habit. Start small, and gradually pace your way up to that 50% mark.

Summary

- **The Treadmill:** The Hedonic Treadmill keeps you running faster just to stay in the exact same financial spot.
- **The Trap:** Parkinson's Law ensures that your expenses will always rise to drain whatever new income you generate.
- **The Escape Plan:** The 50% Rule allows you to enjoy your success today while simultaneously buying your freedom for tomorrow. If 50% feels intimidating, start with 20% and gradually pace your way up.

Action Step: The Appraisal Audit

Look back at your last two salary increments. Calculate exactly how much your monthly income went up. Now, be brutally honest and check: how much did your monthly SIP or savings go up?

Write down the numbers in the table below and come back after your next increment to track your progress:

Increment Amount	Net Savings

"Without accumulation of capital, no big enterprise or investment can ever begin. Even a mountain is formed by small particles of dust coming together."

— Chanakya

"It's not how much money you make, but how much money you keep, how hard it works for you, and how many generations you keep it for."

— Robert T. Kiyosaki

5.

The Toxic Myth: "Saving Se Ameer Nahi Bante"

Busting the social media influencer trap

If you spend even ten minutes on the internet today, you will inevitably hear a *'finfluencer'* shouting this exact phrase at you: *"Savers are losers! Saving money will never make you rich; you have to invest!"*

Technically, they are telling you a half-truth. It is true that simply hoarding cash in a savings account while inflation rises is a losing game. But this half-truth has completely destroyed the financial mindset of our generation. Young earners hear this and develop an absolute hatred for the boring act of saving money.

They rationalize their poor financial habits by thinking, *"If saving ₹10,000 a month isn't going to make me the next Ambani, why bother? I might as well blow it on Zomato Gold, premium OTT subscriptions, and weekend parties."* Everyone wants to talk about the magic of compounding, crypto breakouts, and index funds. But they completely miss the fundamental law of wealth: **Before you can multiply money, you actually have to retain money.** You cannot multiply zero.

The "Knowledgeable" Broke Investor

Meet Raman Verma. Raman is a walking encyclopedia of modern finance.

He listens to all the top financial podcasts, reads the business news, and constantly argues with his parents—mocking their old-school Fixed Deposit (FD) mindset. His favorite defense for his lifestyle is repeating the internet's favorite line: *"Saving se ameer nahi bante (You don't get rich by saving)."*

Because Raman doesn't respect the core concept of saving, he never bothers to control his expenses. He freely spends on Swiggy deliveries, constantly reloads his digital coffee cards just to maintain his "Tier Status," and books expensive cabs everywhere he goes. He lives a 100% lifestyle.

Then, the inevitable happens. A massive stock market crash occurs. The news is panicking, red arrows are everywhere, and stocks are available at a massive discount. It is the absolute perfect time to make a lumpsum investment!

But Raman has a massive problem. He checks his bank account, and after his monthly EMIs and expenses he has exactly ₹863 to invest, which is practically a near zero capital for investment. He possesses all the financial knowledge in the world, but he lacks the one thing required to use it: Capital.

The Seed vs. The Soil

We need to understand the relationship between saving and investing.

Investing is the fertile soil, but saving is the seed. You can have the most nutrient-rich, perfect soil in the world, but if you do not plant a seed, a tree will never grow.

Let's look at the brutal math of zero capital:

- **Scenario A (The Knowledgeable Spender):** Raman waits for the perfect market conditions, identifies the best stock, and generates a legendary 20% return. But his saved capital is just ₹863. And his legendary 20% profit on ₹863 is a mere ₹172.
- **Scenario B (The Boring Saver):** An average investor doesn't know much about the stock market. They simply generate a decent 12% return in a standard index fund. But they had the discipline to save ₹20,000 every single month. That is ₹2.4 Lakhs of pure capital planted into the soil every year.

A 100% return on zero rupees is still zero. Capital allocation is useless if you don't master capital creation first.

Defense Wins Championships

In the financial game, earning money is your offense, but saving money is your defense. You need both to survive.

My favorite legendary boxer Muhammad Ali once famously said, *"The fight is won or lost far away from witnesses—behind the lines, in the gym, and out there on the road, long before I dance under those lights."*

In your financial life, investing is the flashy knockout that everyone watches under the bright lights. It looks cool, it gets the applause, and it makes you look smart. But saving? Saving is the boring, unglamorous gym work that happens early in the morning when no one is watching. If you don't put in the hours at the gym (saving), you will get knocked out in the ring—no matter how hard you can punch (earn).

We need to completely redefine what saving means. Saving is not about "depriving yourself of happiness." Saving is simply the act of **"Paying Yourself First."**

- ❖ For decades, the middle-class mindset formula for money has been:

Income - Expenses = Savings

(You spend first, and save whatever is left over, which is usually nothing).

- ❖ To build real wealth, you must aggressively flip this to the wealthy mindset formula:

Income - Savings (Investments) = Expenses

(You pay your future-self first, and then freely spend whatever is left without any guilt).

Summary

- **The Toxic Myth:** Finfluencers sell the exciting half-truth of investing, but they fail to teach the boring, essential discipline of saving.
- **The Seed and the Soil:** You cannot multiply zero. Financial knowledge is useless without the capital required to execute it.
- **Pay Yourself First:** Earning is your offense, but saving is your defense. The wealthy save first and spend second.

Action Step: The Next-Day Mandate

You do not need willpower; you need a system. Set up an automated bank transfer right now. The moment your salary hits your account, schedule an automated transfer for the *very next day*. A fixed percentage (be it 20%, 15%, 10% or even 5%) of your income must immediately move to a separate investment account before you buy a single coffee, order a single meal, or pay a single bill.

Right now, the exact percentage does not matter. What matters is building the habit. This single action will shift your perspective, helping you defeat the 'poor mindset' you have been conditioned with since birth, and finally build a system for true wealth.

"A clear conscience is the softest pillow. You cannot sleep peacefully if your lifestyle is funded by borrowed money."

— N.R. Narayana Murthy

"If you buy things you do not need, soon you will have to sell things you need."

— Warren Buffett

6.

The EMI Millionaires

Buying Liabilities to Fuel the Lifestyle

There has been a massive, silent shift in the middle-class mindset over the last decade. Ten years ago (2016), if someone wanted to buy a flagship phone, they would look at the price tag and ask themselves: "Can I afford to spend ₹1 Lakh on a phone?". Today, nobody looks at the total price. Thanks to the explosion of "Buy Now, Pay Later" (BNPL) and "No-Cost EMI" schemes, the question has completely changed to: "Can I afford to pay ₹8,000 a month?".

This simple psychological trick has created a brand-new species in our society: The EMI Millionaires. If you look at their Instagram profiles, they look incredibly wealthy. They flaunt the latest iPhone Pro Max, a premium smartwatch, limited-edition sneakers, and an Insta story with a trending song recording them behind the wheel of their shiny new SUV. But beneath the surface, they do not actually own any of it—the bank owns their lifestyle. They have unknowingly become indentured servants, trading their future time and freedom just to look rich today.

The "Rich" Beggar Let's look at the life of Aryan Sharma. Aryan is a senior software developer earning a very handsome in-hand salary of ₹1,30,000 per month. When he walks into his office with Apple AirPods Pro in his ears, smelling of expensive cologne, wearing a brand-screaming shirt paired with limited-edition sneakers, and holding his everyday Starbucks coffee—he looks like the absolute definition of success.

But Aryan's month does not belong to him. On the 2nd of every month, his phone continuously buzzes with automated bank deductions:

- ₹32,000 for the shiny SUV.
- ₹7,584 for his latest iPhone.
- ₹6,749 for the massive OLED TV in his living room.

- ₹8,500 for a personal loan he took to fund his "aesthetic" Bali vacation.

Out of his ₹1,30,000 salary, ₹54,833 vanishes instantly. His month hasn't even started, yet 42% of his income is already gone. Now, he has to manage his rent, groceries, fuel, and weekend outings with whatever is left. By the end of the month, after all the lifestyle expenses are made, the final amount left in Aryan's bank account is a tragic ₹3,683.

Aryan isn't working for himself, and he certainly isn't working for his future. Mathematically, he is working 13 days every single month just as a free employee for the banks. Despite his high salary, Aryan is exactly one medical emergency or one bad appraisal away from total bankruptcy.

The "No-Cost" Illusion & Opportunity Cost How did smart people like Aryan fall into this trap?. Through the greatest marketing scam of the 21st century—the "No-Cost EMI". Retailers and credit card companies make you believe you are paying 0% interest. But let's break down the brutal, hidden math of a ₹1,54,900 flagship phone bought on a 24-month "No-Cost EMI" of ₹7,584 per month.

First, the banks will quietly add hidden charges:

- **File Processing Fee:** ₹299.
- **GST (18% on the hidden interest component):** ₹4,934.
- **The Loss of Upfront Cash Discount:** If you bought the phone with upfront cash, the dealer was offering a ₹5,232 discount. Because you chose EMI, you lost this money.

You didn't just pay ₹1,54,900. You paid significantly more in invisible fees and lost discounts. But the real tragedy is the Opportunity Cost. Renowned Indian financial minds, like Raamdeo Agrawal, Chairman and Co-founder of Motilal Oswal

Group, constantly remind investors about the 8th wonder of the world: Compounding. When you invest, compounding works for you. But when you take an EMI for a depreciating asset, you are putting compounding in reverse gear.

If Aryan didn't have that phone EMI, and instead invested that ₹7,584 every month into a simple index fund for the next 10 years, that money would have grown to nearly ₹17 Lakhs. By trying to look cool today, Aryan didn't just buy a ₹1.5 Lakh phone—he paid an invisible tax of ₹17 Lakhs from his future wealth. He paid with his future freedom.

The RBI Warning: A Nation on EMI If you think this trap is just an individual problem, look at the national data. The Reserve Bank of India (RBI) has repeatedly raised massive red flags regarding this exact middle-class illusion. According to RBI's financial stability metrics, unsecured retail loans—which include consumer durables, credit cards, and personal loans primarily used for lifestyle upgrades—have surged at an alarming rate of 25% to 30% year-on-year.

This debt accumulation is growing at more than double the speed of normal salary increments. The situation became so dangerously inflated that the RBI was forced to heavily increase the "risk weights" on unsecured consumer loans simply to penalize and discourage banks from handing out easy EMIs to individuals. When the central bank of a country has to actively step in to stop citizens from taking on too much lifestyle debt, you know the "EMI Millionaire" epidemic has become a terrifying national crisis.

Disguising Liabilities as Assets In India today, selling a liability by disguising it as an asset has become a multi-billion dollar business. Brands don't just sell you products anymore; they sell you emotions. They test your ego, they leverage peer pressure, and they trap you in the fear of missing out. If you cannot differentiate between an asset and a liability, you will always be a victim of these traps.

The core definition is brutally simple: An asset is something that puts money into your pocket. A liability is something that takes money out of your pocket. When a car salesman emotionally convinces you that a ₹32 Lakh SUV is a "great asset for your family's status," he is playing with your ego. That car will lose value the second you drive it out of the showroom, and it will keep taking money out of your pocket for fuel, maintenance, and EMIs. It is a pure liability disguised as an achievement.

Redefining Affordability Top Indian financial planners like Kirtan Shah often emphasize the critical difference between "Good Debt" and "Bad Debt". Taking a home loan makes mathematical sense because a house is an Asset, it generally appreciates in value over time. But taking an EMI for a phone, a TV, a car, or a vacation is buying a Liability. It is financial suicide because the moment you buy it, its value drops, while you keep paying for it for years.

To escape this trap, we need to shift to a new definition of "affordability"—from monthly payments to total wealth impact. We must adopt the famous golden rule coined by billionaire rapper Jay-Z: "If you can't buy it twice (in cash), you can't afford it". If you have ₹1,50,000 in your bank account, you cannot afford a ₹1,00,000 phone. Why? Because buying it would wipe out 66% of your net worth. You can only afford that phone if you have ₹2,00,000 or more saved up explicitly for lifestyle purchases.

Summary

- **The EMI Trap:** EMIs disguise liabilities as assets. They trick your brain into focusing on the small monthly payment rather than the massive total cost.
- **The "No-Cost" Myth:** There is no such thing as zero interest. You pay through processing fees, GST on hidden interest, and lost cash discounts.
- **The National Debt Crisis:** Unsecured EMIs are growing at a 25-30% rate, forcing the RBI to actively warn the nation and tighten banking rules.
- **Jay-Z's Rule:** Stop buying depreciating assets on loan. If you cannot comfortably buy the item twice in pure cash, you cannot afford it. Don't take it on your ego—you are only hurting your future self.

Action Step: The DTI (Debt-to-Income) Audit

It is time for a brutal reality check. In the banking world, this is called the FOIR (Fixed Obligation to Income Ratio). In India, the golden rule of personal finance dictates that your total overall EMIs (including a home loan) should never exceed 40% of your take-home salary.

However, for *unsecured lifestyle debt*, the rules are much stricter.

Write down every single EMI you are currently paying (Car, Phone, TV, Personal Loans—exclude *your Home Loan*). Divide that total EMI amount by your monthly in-hand salary to find your "Lifestyle Debt Ratio."

If your Lifestyle Debt Ratio is above 15%, you are in the danger zone. You need to declare a financial emergency, stop all discretionary spending, and focus aggressively on clearing this bad debt.

"There are no get-rich-quick schemes. That's just someone else getting rich off you."

— Naval Ravikant

"Investing should be more like watching paint dry or watching grass grow. If you want excitement, take your money and go to Las Vegas."

— Paul Samuelson

7.
The "21 Din Mein Paisa Double" Trap

The deadly race for quick wealth & options trading

Remember the iconic Bollywood movie *Phir Hera Pheri*? The character Raju is blinded by the greed of doubling his money in 21 days (*"21 din mein paisa double"*). To fund this get-rich-quick scheme, he takes extreme leverage by borrowing money from a ruthless underworld don. When the shady scheme inevitably bursts, Raju doesn't just lose his money—he drags his entire family into a massive, life-threatening trap.

Bring this to the 21st century. Today, you do not need to meet a scammer in a dark alley to destroy your life. The modern-day underworld dons are sitting right inside your smartphone—they come in the form of Telegram channels, WhatsApp "tip" groups, and flashy YouTube ads promising "₹10,000 daily guaranteed profit."

And the ultimate wealth destroyer of our generation? Futures & Options (F&O) trading—fueled by borrowed money.

The "Apun Ich Bhagwaan Hai" Tragedy

Meet Varun Bhel, a 23 year-old professional. Like millions of young Indians, Varun opened a Demat account, discovered the fast-paced world of F&O trading, and placed a few trades. By sheer dumb luck, Varun made a quick profit.

This beginner's luck is the worst thing that can happen to a young investor. It triggers the *"Apun ich bhagwaan hai"* (God Complex). Varun started believing he was a financial genius who had successfully hacked the hidden matrix of the stock market—something even the greatest experts before him couldn't crack.

But the market is a ruthless teacher. Soon, the inevitable first big loss hit him. Instead of accepting the loss and stepping back, Varun's ego took over—and he entered the deadly psychological phase of "Revenge Trading." He desperately wanted his money back from the market. To multiply his bets, he took massive leverage (margin) from his broker. When that wasn't enough to cover his growing losses, he maxed out his credit cards and took personal loans from friends and digital loan apps.

Eventually, the market did what it always does to gamblers: it wiped him out completely.

The climax of Varun's story is not just a financial loss—it is a generational horror story. The debt became so incredibly massive that his retired father's entire life savings of ₹3 Crores, money earned over 40 brutal years of sweating and sacrificing, were completely wiped out just to pay off the angry lenders.

And the nightmare doesn't end there. They *still* have a ₹4 Crore debt pending. Today, the retired father is forced to work a ₹30,000 job at an old age just to survive, while Varun is grinding away at two different jobs—one during the day and another in the evening—making ₹25,000 and ₹10,000 respectively. One young man's greed for quick money sentenced his entire family to lifetime financial slavery.

The Mathematics of Ruin (Leverage & The SEBI Reality)

Let's understand the silent killer that destroyed Varun—Leverage (or Margin).

Suppose you have ₹10,000. Your broker generously offers you a 10x margin, allowing you to execute a trade worth ₹1,00,000. It sounds like a superpower. If the market goes up by just 5%, you make ₹5,000. That is a massive 50% return on your actual ₹10,000 capital in a single day!

BUT, here is the fatal catch—if the market drops by just 10%, your loss is ₹10,000. Your entire actual capital is wiped out to absolute ZERO in a matter of seconds.

If you think you are smart enough to beat these odds, look at the brutal reality check provided by SEBI (Securities and Exchange Board of India). Their official report states a chilling truth: **9 out**

of 10 individual traders in the equity F&O segment lose money.

When you trade F&O, you are not competing against other average retail guys. You are fighting a war against institutional supercomputers, high-frequency algorithmic bots, and billionaires who have armies of analysts. The math is completely rigged against you.

Wealth is a Crockpot, Not a Microwave

We need a desperate shift in our expectations. You must transition your mindset from the "Get Rich Quick" fantasy to the "Get Wealthy Slowly" reality.

The stock market is not a casino designed for your entertainment—it is an ownership machine designed to build long-term wealth. Real investing is actually supposed to be incredibly boring. If your investing is giving you adrenaline rushes, sweaty palms, and heart palpitations, you are not investing—you are GAMBLING!

To protect yourself and your future family from becoming the next Varun, you must establish one non-negotiable life rule—**Never, ever invest borrowed money.**

Summary

- **The Hera Pheri Trap:** "21 din mein paisa double" is always a scam. Quick money always leads to quick ruin.
- **The God Complex:** Beginner's luck in F&O leads to overconfidence, which inevitably results in revenge trading and taking on toxic debt.
- **The Dynamite of Leverage:** Leverage amplifies your profits, but it also accelerates your losses to zero. You cannot beat the 90% failure rate in F&O.

Action Step: The Casino Block

This is a highly practical emergency step. Open your broker's app or log into your Demat account settings right now. Find the "Segment Activation" section and manually **Deactivate the F&O / Derivatives segment**.

Next, open your messaging apps and delete every single Telegram channel or WhatsApp group that promises "sure-shot stock tips" or "daily profits." Cut off the toxic supply of gambling triggers from your life today.

"If you secretly despise wealth, it will elude you."

— Naval Ravikant

"Whether you think you can, or you think you can't – you're right."

— Henry Ford

8.

The Middle-Class Guilt

Why we subconsciously sabotage our own wealth

Walk into any average Indian middle-class household at dinner time, and you will observe a fascinating pattern. On the dining table, the family will happily discuss national politics, cricket matches, neighborhood gossip, and inevitably compare their children to the legendary *"Sharma Ji ka beta."* But there is one topic that is strictly banned from the dining table—**Money**.

In our society, talking openly about money is considered 'greedy' or 'unsanskari' (lacking values). Because of this profound silence, a child's entire financial programming is built on negative, scarcity-driven taunts. From a very young age, whenever we ask for something, we are hit with phrases like:

- *"Paise ped par nahi ugte!" (Money doesn't grow on trees)*
- *"Apni aukat mein rehna seekho." (Stay within your limits)*
- *"Tum paise ki bahut hiras karte ho." (You are too greedy for money)*
- *"Humein zyada lalach nahi karna chahiye." (We shouldn't be too ambitious)*

By the time we grow up, our subconscious mind has been deeply programmed to treat money as an evil entity that destroys human values. We are taught to subconsciously repel wealth.

The "Chadar" Syndrome & The Bitter Critic

Let's look at how this childhood programming ruins adulthood by following the life of Sameer Kalra.

Sameer grew up in a household heavily dominated by the scarcity mindset of his father, Ramesh. Ramesh believed in only one financial strategy—ruthlessly cutting expenses. He never focused on upskilling or growing his income. If young Sameer ever demanded a new toy or a trip, Ramesh would immediately scold him and bitterly count every single penny he had spent on

Sameer's upbringing. Furthermore, whenever Ramesh saw a former colleague or neighbor becoming wealthy, he would openly curse them in front of the family, declaring, *"He must have done something illegal. You cannot make that kind of money with honesty."*

Sameer absorbed this exact blueprint. He grew up believing the most famous Indian middle-class half-truth: *"Jitni chadar ho, utne hi pair failaane chahiye"* (Only stretch your legs as much as your blanket allows).

Sameer follows this advice blindly. He constantly cuts expenses, avoids vacations, and lives far below his means. But he completely ignores the second, hidden, and more important part of this truth—**You must continuously work to buy a bigger blanket.**

Because Sameer never focused on his income growth, he feels financially suffocated. One day at the office, he sees a colleague driving a brand-new luxury car. Instead of being inspired or curious about how the colleague achieved it, Sameer's middle-class guilt and childhood programming kick in. He automatically whispers, *"Zaroor isne do number ka (illegal) kaam kiya hoga, imandaari se itna paisa nahi banta."* Sameer judges the rich simply to feel better about his own financial stagnation.

The Mathematical Limit of Cutting Expenses

Why did Sameer's extreme frugality fail to make him wealthy? Because focusing only on the "Chadar" (cutting expenses) is mathematically flawed.

There is a mathematical floor to how much you can save. If you earn ₹50,000 a month, you can ruthlessly cut your expenses to ₹20,000 and save ₹30,000. But you cannot cut your expenses to zero. Savings generated purely by cutting expenses have a strict mathematical limit.

However, there is absolutely no mathematical ceiling to how much you can earn. Your income can go from ₹50,000 to ₹1 Lakh, and eventually to ₹5 Lakhs. Relying only on frugality is a slow, painful game; pairing frugality with continuous income growth is the real formula for wealth.

The Reality Hit

Here is the most terrifying part. When you hear that India has an average annual inflation rate of 6% to 7%, you are only looking at a comforting half-truth. That is just the *general* inflation for basic groceries and daily goods. The real silent killers are lurking elsewhere.

Education inflation in India is growing at a massive 12% to 14% annually. Medical inflation is also skyrocketing at 12% to 14%. Add to that a subconscious lifestyle inflation of 3% to 5% as society upgrades around you. When you combine these, the actual, real-world inflation hitting a middle-class family is well over 10% to 12%.

If your annual income growth does not aggressively beat this number, it doesn't matter how many expenses you brutally cut—inflation will eventually catch up to you. It will completely choke your purchasing power, and you will feel an unbearable financial suffocation. This could hit you in your mid-50s, or even worse, during your mid-60s and early 70s when you can no longer work, and a single medical bill can wipe out your lifetime of savings. Relying strictly on extreme frugality without income growth is a guaranteed path to poverty.

Money DOES Grow on Trees

It is time to demolish the biggest middle-class myth of all time. We were lied to when our elders told us, "Money doesn't grow on trees."

The absolute truth is: **Money absolutely grows on trees—provided you know how to become a financial farmer.**

If you want to grow a wealth tree, here is the exact agricultural process:

- **The Seed:** Your regular monthly savings, planted mechanically through an **SIP (Systematic Investment Plan)**.
- **The Soil:** The highly fertile land of the stock market, mutual funds, bonds, Gold/Silver, Real Estate or even FDs/RDs.
- **The Time & Water:** Your ultimate superpower—patience and the magic of compounding. You must let the seed endure the changing seasons of the market.
- **The Fruits:** After a decade or two, once the tree is fully grown and deeply rooted, you do not chop it down. You simply sit under its shade and eat the fresh fruits forever using the **SWP (Systematic Withdrawal Plan)** method.

Summary

- **The Money Taboo:** Treating money as an "unsanskari" or evil topic programs your subconscious mind to repel wealth and resent successful people.
- **The Mathematical Floor:** "Jitni chadar" is a half-truth. There is a limit to how much you can cut your expenses, but there is no limit to how much you can grow your income. Beating inflation requires growth, not just savings.
- **The Wealth Tree:** Money does grow on trees. You just have to plant the seed of SIP in fertile soil and harvest it later with SWP.

Action Step: The Dining Table Audit

Tonight, break the generational curse. Have an open, honest conversation about money at your dining table. Define and discuss a specific financial goal—whether it's a retirement corpus, a vacation fund, or paying off a debt—with your spouse or your parents, completely free of guilt or shame.

Treat money as a tool for freedom, not a taboo.

"Mixing insurance with investment is the biggest financial mistake Indians make. You end up with neither adequate protection nor real wealth."

— Nithin Kamath

"In investing, what is comfortable is rarely profitable."

— Robert Arnott

9. The "Safe" Investment Illusion

The dark psychology behind falling for LICs, ULIPs, and FDs

Think back to the days of your childhood. Do you remember when your family's 'favorite uncle' or a close family friend would walk into your drawing room carrying a thick leather diary and a calculator? They presented themselves as trusted "Financial Advisors," but in reality, they were just high-commission salesmen.

They served Indian middle-class families a toxic financial dish, a chaotic mixture of 'Insurance' and 'Investment.' They pitched it as the *"Best of Both Worlds"*. In truth, this combination is the ***worst in the world***. It provides neither a substantial life cover nor inflation-beating returns. These agents simply mesmerized families by flashing a large absolute number: *"Sir, just deposit ₹5 Lakhs today, and you will get ₹10 Lakhs after twenty years!"* While ten lakhs sounds massive to a middle-class earner, if you calculate the actual CAGR (Compound Annual Growth Rate), it often turns out to be lower than a basic bank FD.

The Tax-Saving Loop & The Missing Maturity

Meet Rajeev Saxena. Rajeev is a 63-year-old teacher at a senior secondary school in Ghaziabad.

Every year when March arrived, Rajeev faced immense pressure to save taxes. If there is one thing that magnetically attracts the Indian middle class, it is the phrase 'Tax Saving.' Capitalizing on this exact mindset, that same Agent uncle would conveniently show up and hand him a new endowment policy or a trending ULIP. Once Rajeev became a customer, he was locked into an endless loop—a new policy pushed onto him every single year.

Because of these heavy, recurring premiums, Rajeev's monthly in-hand salary was choked to the point where he barely had enough money left for daily household expenses. Yet, he consoled himself by thinking, *"At least a massive corpus will be ready when my daughter needs her college fees."*

Years later, when his daughter was ready for college and Rajeev approached the company for the maturity amount, he received a brutal shock. Instead of a fortune, he was handed mere 'chillar.' The agent who used to say, *"Sir, you just move forward, we are right behind you,"* suddenly changed his tune completely. The stance shifted to: *"Move along, just keep paying your premiums on time."* Using a minor technicality or a single missed premium as an excuse, the company swallowed the chunk of his expected returns, leaving a trusting middle-class investor completely stranded.

The 25% Secret & ULIP's "Capital Guarantee" Scam

Why do agents push these traditional insurance policies so aggressively? Let us unveil their darkest secret: the commission structure.

An agent's first-year commission can be as high as **25%** of your annual premium, and sometimes even more when festival bonuses are included! In the second and third years, they pocket 7.5% annually, and from the fourth year onwards, they continue to receive around 5% of your premium every single year. Essentially, an agent sits back and makes money as long as you blindly keep paying your premiums. Does this trigger a memory? Has this exact setup happened to you or your parents?

Then came ULIPs and "Return of Premium" (Capital Guarantee) plans—nothing but old traps packaged in modern, shiny wrappers. They pitch it with a clever psychological trap: *"Look, in a normal term plan, if you survive past the age of 65, all your money goes to waste. But in our plan, your entire premium will be safely returned to you!"* Blinded by this illusion of getting their money back, the middle class completely ignores the heavy mortality charges and allocation fees.

Let us look at the raw, undisputed math. Suppose a 25-year-old individual wants a ₹1 Crore life cover until the age of 65 (a 40-year tenure):

- **Scenario A: The Return of Premium Plan (The Trap)**
  - Annual Premium: Approximately ₹18,000.
  - Total premium paid over 40 years: ₹7,20,000.
  - At age 65, the company proudly returns your exact principal: **₹7,20,000**.
- **Scenario B: Pure Term Plan + Index Fund (The Wealth Machine)**
  - A ₹1 Crore Pure Term Insurance plan costs an annual premium of around ₹9,000.
  - By choosing this, you instantly save ₹9,000 a year (which is ₹750 a month).
  - Now, route this saved ₹750 every month into a Systematic Investment Plan (SIP) in a Nifty 50 Index Fund.
  - At age 65, assuming a conservative historical return of 12% CAGR, this tiny monthly SIP compounds into a staggering: **Approx ₹88,00,000 (88 Lakhs)!**

On one side, you have ₹7.2 Lakhs. On the other side, you have ₹88 Lakhs. By playing on your ego and fear of "losing premium," the agent quietly stripped away over ₹80 Lakhs of your future wealth. *(Note: Index funds are market-linked instruments, meaning past performance does not guarantee 100% fixed future returns. However, historical data heavily demonstrates that long-term equity investing consistently multiplies wealth).*

FDs are a Parking Lot, Not a Wealth Engine

Now, let us tackle the most sacred financial instrument of our parents' generation: Fixed Deposits (FDs) and Recurring Deposits (RDs).

In their era, an FD was a magnificent **Wealth Engine**. The economic landscape was entirely different; inflation was controlled, and FDs comfortably yielded 9% to 12% interest. The old adage was legendary: "Put your money in an FD, and it will double in 6 to 7 years"—thanks to the famous Rule of 72.

But as the Indian economy matured, banks grew larger, inflation shifted, and FD interest rates systematically cratered. Today, bank FD interest rates hover around a meager 6% to 6.5%.

The Harsh Reality: At a pre-tax level, a 6% FD barely keeps its head above inflation. Once you factor in your income tax slab, the post-tax return of an FD actually loses money against real-world inflation. Your purchasing power is systematically dying inside a fixed deposit.

This means the role of the FD has fundamentally transformed. It is no longer a **Wealth Engine**; it has become a **Wealth Engine Protector**.

Fixed deposits are not meant to make you rich. They are designed to absorb financial shocks so that you never have to disrupt your actual wealth-building engines (like mutual funds, index funds, or high-dividend stocks) during a crisis. In today's era, an FD is merely a safe parking lot for your short-term emergency funds—a safety net, not a wealth creation factory. This is the exact mathematical truth that older generations fail to see, leading to endless arguments at home over why FDs are simply not enough anymore.

Summary

- **The Toxic Mix:** Combining insurance and investment makes you poor and your agent rich. Labeling these policies as the "Best of Both Worlds" is a half-truth designed to benefit the corporation, not the policyholder.
- **The Tax Illusion:** Never let the desperation of saving taxes choke your monthly cash flow into illiquid, low-yielding assets.
- **The FD Evolution:** Fixed deposits have transitioned from being wealth creators to wealth protectors. Use them exclusively as an emergency shield, not a growth vehicle.

Action Step: The Portfolio Cleansing

Draw a strict line between your protection and your investments today. Secure your family's future by purchasing a Pure Term Insurance plan with an adequate cover. Take the remaining amount you were wasting on traditional premiums and automate a monthly SIP into direct Mutual Funds or Index Funds. Calculate the actual CAGR of your existing traditional policies, face the real numbers, and liberate your trapped capital.

"We have to shift from physical savings to financial savings to truly build the economy and our wealth."

— Raghuram Rajan

"Never fall in love with an asset. It won't love you back."

— Wall Street Adage

10. Eenth, Sona Aur Cash Ka Sach

The emotional trap of dead real estate and physical gold

In India, you are not considered truly successful until you own a piece of land—bricks—and have a bank locker filled with that yellow metal—gold. For our parents' generation, these two are not just investments; they are the ultimate matrix to measure status and respect in society. We buy these assets not by looking at cold, hard math, but out of pure emotion and societal pressure. And the moment emotion enters finance, math is the first to jump out of the window.

The Ultimate Symbol of Prestige (And the Game of Show-Off)

Building a home is the ultimate lifelong dream of every middle-class individual. If we look back at the 1980s and 1990s, the ratio between an average man's salary and property prices was quite comfortable. People could easily buy a decent home from their savings. But today, in 2026, the situation has completely inverted. Today, if a young earner making ₹25,000 a month wants to buy a flat in a decent locality, the prices start at no less than ₹50 to ₹60 Lakhs. These days, it is not just the height of the buildings that is rising in cities—their prices are touching the sky as well.

On top of these skyrocketing prices enters the biggest modern scam of our system—Home Loans. Globally and mathematically, the rule is crystal clear: your total monthly EMIs should never exceed 40% of your take-home salary to maintain a healthy financial status. But loan-selling corporations have completely twisted this concept.

When you visit a property dealer or a bank executive, they target your deepest insecurities. They approve EMIs that consume 65% to 75% of your take-home salary, behaving like your ultimate well-wisher: "Sir, I got this deal approved specially for you with a custom clearance!"

But the reality is exactly the opposite. They have trapped you in a heavy, suffocating EMI loop that turns you into a slave to the bank for the next 20 to 30 years. After paying this massive chunk, you are left with so little money that you can never make early prepayments to clear the debt. When you sign a home loan contract, you aren't just giving away your current money—you are signing away the next 30 years of your future earnings to the bank.

And what is all this for? Purely for show-off and vanity. In India, a house has become the ultimate vehicle for social display—imported Italian marble flooring, a high-tech modular kitchen, and a larger-than-life lavish living area cluttered with souvenirs from foreign trips. When a guest walks in, the host desperately wants them to notice and ask about these things. Then, the host blushes a little, acts modest, and subtly drops: "Oh this? I picked this up during my trip to Spain last month. And that artifact over there? I brought it from the USA six months ago." In a single, unsolicited statement, they have subtly broadcasted that they traveled to both Spain and the USA within six months!

Corporations understand this game of vanity deeply. All their marketing campaigns target your insecurities and ego, forcing you to step out of your financial comfort zone, fall into their loan traps, and hand over your present and future wealth to them.

But the bitterest truth is that the house you are leveraging to show off isn't even technically yours. Until the very last EMI is paid, the bank is the true owner of that house. You are just one medical emergency or one job loss away from bankruptcy and foreclosure. And the saddest part? The friends, relatives, and neighbors you invited to throw lavish parties for and display your status—when the bank puts up an auction board and evicts you, not a single one of them will come to your rescue. Instead, that same society will mock you behind your back: "He used to fly too high, always showing off. Look at him now, brought straight back to reality. The bank showed him his true worth."

Asset-Rich, Cash-Poor

Meet Prakash Sharma, a senior advocate in Delhi with 35 years of experience. Prakash earns a handsome amount annually, and his entire financial worldview revolves around hoarding physical assets.

Prakash put all his life savings into buying a second residential flat for "rental income," tying himself to a heavy monthly EMI. Alongside this, whatever little money he had left over each month, he systematically bought physical gold jewelry to stack in a bank locker for his daughter's future wedding. Sitting in his living room, Prakash felt like a king. On paper, his net worth crossed ₹2 Crores.

Then, one day, an unexpected and massive medical emergency struck the family. The doctor delivered a brutal mandate: ₹25 Lakhs in pure cash was required within the next 48 hours for an urgent operation.

Prakash rushed into the market to liquidate his second flat. But the real estate market was stagnant, buyers ruthlessly lowballed him seeing his desperation, and brokers warned that the paperwork alone would take months. Panicked, Prakash turned to the gold locker, but his family emotionally resisted, protesting that it was their daughter's 'streedhan' and could not be touched.

When he finally managed to take the jewelry to a local goldsmith, the jeweler deducted 20% of the value instantly under the guise of making charges and melting losses. Prakash realized a terrifying truth that day: he was a multi-millionaire on paper, but a complete beggar when a real-life crisis demanded immediate cash.

The Illusion of "Price Appreciation"

Let us decode the hidden math that your local property dealer and jeweler systematically keep hidden from you.

Real Estate Reality

There is a massive myth in the middle class that "property prices always go up." Suppose you buy a flat worth ₹1 Crore. The average residential rental yield in India is a meager 2% to 3% annually. This means a ₹1 Crore house brings in barely ₹2 to ₹3 Lakhs a year in rent. Once you subtract property tax, society maintenance, vacant months, and the horrific interest on the home loan, the actual inflation-adjusted CAGR of real estate barely hovers around 6% to 8%. This completely shatters the illusion of "multiplying your money 10x in 10 years."

Physical Gold Reality

When you buy gold jewelry thinking it is your safest investment, corporations smile behind closed doors. Gold jewelry carries heavy making charges ranging from 15% to 20%, plus an additional 3% GST. This means the exact second you step out of the jewelry showroom, the investment value of your gold plummets by 20% to 30% into the negative! You are starting an investment where you take an instant 25% hit on day one. Add to this the risk of purity, the fear of theft, and recurring locker charges.

Note: Buying gold is not wrong, but calling jewelry an investment is a profound mistake. If wealth creation is your goal, Sovereign Gold Bonds (SGBs) or Gold Mutual Funds/ETFs are infinitely better options—offering zero making charges, zero GST, and an additional 2.5% guaranteed annual interest (SGBs).

Liquidity is King

Is a house an asset or a liability? Financial experts worldwide have highly conflicting views on this. But the truth is, you should view your primary home neither as a pure asset nor a pure liability.

Owning the primary house you live in provides immense mental peace. It frees you from the landlord's interference and the constant anxiety of annual rent hikes. On the flip side, buying a house locks up a massive portion of your net worth in a single geographic location forever. In times of distress, you cannot sell a single room, a floor, or a marble tile to raise money. Real estate comes with a severe liquidity trap.

Therefore, there is no "one size fits all" rule for buying a home. You must balance it based on your unique financial health. While a primary home is an emotional necessity, buying a second flat on EMI for a meager 2% rental yield is pure financial suicide.

We must aggressively shift our mindset from hoarding dead, illiquid assets to accumulating productive, liquid assets. If you need ₹2 Lakhs tomorrow morning, you can liquidate your Index Funds or Mutual Funds via your smartphone in exactly three clicks, bringing cash straight to your bank account. In a crisis, liquidity is your only true savior.

Summary

- **The Loan Slavery:** When you allocate more than 40% of your take-home income toward EMIs, you willingly sign a contract to become a slave to the bank for 30 years.
- **The Show-off Cost:** The price of the luxury house and high-end interiors we display to society is paid with our future freedom. Society only stands by your vanity, never your emergencies.
- **The Jewelry Math:** Buying gold jewelry immediately devalues your investment by 20-30% due to making charges and taxes. Treat it as a lifestyle luxury, never a core investment.

Action Step: The Liquidity Audit

Tonight, conduct a brutal financial audit. Calculate your total net worth, but exclude the primary residence you live in (since you will never realistically sell it). Now, look at what percentage of your remaining wealth is locked inside physical real estate and gold jewelry. If this number exceeds 50%, you are exposed to a massive liquidity risk. Redirect all future savings into highly liquid financial instruments—Mutual Funds, Index Funds, Gold ETFs/SGBs and Stocks—ensuring that while you are wealthy on paper, your pockets remain permanently full of cash.

"Simplicity is the ultimate sophistication. You don't need a heavy price tag to prove your worth."

— Sudha Murty

"We spend our whole lives waiting for the right moment, and then we blow it all on one party."

— F. Scott Fitzgerald

11.
The Wedding Bankruptcy

Blowing up your net worth for a 3-day PR event

Want to witness the ultimate paradox of the Indian middle class? Look at the parents who live frugally their entire lives. They will bargain relentlessly with the vegetable vendor to save ten rupees, and they will strictly lock the air conditioner at 24 degrees to save on the electricity bill. Yet, the exact moment the word "Marriage" is uttered in the house, all financial sanity completely vanishes. They will willingly bleed their lifetime of savings and pour their hard-earned money literally down the drain.

The "Izzat" Conditioning & The Great Indian Paradox From a very young age, a middle-class child is subconsciously programmed with a toxic financial belief: A wedding is not a union of two people; it is the ultimate test of a family's *Izzat* (prestige) and *Haisiyat* (status).

Parents spend decades living in extreme deprivation, skipping vacations and wearing old clothes, secretly justifying it by thinking, "When my son/daughter gets married, I will show the world who I am." The society conditions them to believe that throwing a massive feast for thousands of people—most of whom they don't even talk to—is the only way to earn respect.

Fast forward to today, and this generational ego has collided with the modern social media culture driven by FOMO, YOLO, and "Fake it till you make it". Weddings have mutated from sacred ceremonies into toxic, commercialized PR events where relationships take a backseat, and expensive sarees, foreign destinations, and designer lehengas do all the talking.

Let's look at how this toxic cocktail of traditional ego and modern vanity ruins a young life by following the story of Gaurav Maan. Gaurav is a 33-year-old Senior Software Engineer from Delhi, working in a high-profile global role for a massive MNC.

Gaurav grew up watching his father, "Maan-saab," live a highly compromised life just to save money. Maan-saab always felt looked down upon by his wealthier relatives. For him, Gaurav's wedding was his lifetime opportunity for revenge—a chance to display his societal status and finally prove his worth to the local community. On the other hand, Gaurav and his fiancée were heavily infected by the "Insta-Perfect" illusion. They didn't want a marriage; they wanted an aesthetic.

When the planning started, both generations fed each other's financial ruin. The extravaganza kicked off with a ₹5 Lakh pre-wedding shoot at an international location. Next came the wedding itself—a grand "Raja-Maharaja" themed destination event hosted inside a massive, historic fort in Rajasthan. His bride purchased a magnificent designer lehenga from a celebrity designer in Mumbai for a staggering ₹10 Lakhs—an outfit explicitly meant to be worn exactly once in a lifetime! She paired it with custom sneakers solely to record a trending reel.

To satisfy Maan-saab's traditional ego, they hosted a colossal grand reception back in Delhi, inviting thousands of guests. To cap off the modern madness, the newlyweds jetted off for a one-week ultra-luxurious honeymoon package in a private water villa in the Maldives, costing roughly ₹11 Lakhs. Combined, these spiraling expenses pushed the total wedding budget to an astronomical ₹75 Lakhs.

The Mathematics of a Social Display On the stage, the newly-weds are smiling beautifully as cameras flash from every direction. But behind Gaurav's calm eyes, a brutal calculator is running inside his brain.

To fund this three-day illusion of luxury, he has taken a massive ₹35 Lakh unsecured Personal Loan. His married life is not starting with romance, peace, or financial security; it is initiating with the crushing weight of EMI anxiety, psychological stress, and suffocating debt.

Let us break down the devastating mathematics behind this social display. Gaurav secured a ₹35 Lakh Personal Loan at a steep 15% interest rate. For the next five years, he is contractually obligated to pay an EMI of approximately ₹83,000 every single month. By the time the loan concludes, the total repayment to the bank will stand at a staggering ₹50 Lakhs!

Consider the sheer opportunity cost of that ₹10 Lakh lehenga and the ₹16 Lakh spent combined on the pre-wedding shoot and the Maldives honeymoon. If Gaurav had ignored the social noise, opted for a graceful, simple wedding, and systematically routed that ₹15 to ₹20 Lakh into a Nifty 50 Index Fund for his new family or used it as a down payment for a home, his next generation would have been financially secure. Instead, he traded ten years of psychological peace to please an ungrateful crowd of relatives and acquaintances who left the reception complaining that the paneer dish lacked adequate salt.

A Wedding is NOT a Marriage We must urgently separate the "Event" from the "Journey." A wedding is merely a fleeting, three-day event, whereas a marriage is a profound 30-to-40-year lifelong journey. Setting fire to the very foundation of a 30-year journey just to fuel a three-day visual show is absolute financial illiteracy. True wealth is silent, while fake wealth is consistently loud. Couples must deliberately drop the toxic urge to outrun their social circle in a race that has no finish line.

Summary

- **The Toxic PR Event:** Modern weddings have transitioned into commercialized PR campaigns. Financing a social media aesthetic through high-interest personal loans sabotages your marriage before it even begins. The ROI of trying to impress society is always absolute zero.
- **The Generational Ego:** Mixing a parent's lifelong desire to "show off" to society with a young couple's social media FOMO creates a financial black hole.
- **The Lehenga Illusion:** Blowing millions on a single day's attire for fleeting online validation is the ultimate form of wealth destruction.

Action Step: The Marriage Start-up Capital

Treat your wedding budget exactly like seed funding for a brand-new start-up—which is your new life together. Sit down with your partner and parents today and firmly establish a strict "No-Debt Wedding Rule." Resolve that only a minor, sensible percentage of your net worth will be allocated to the celebration, and the remaining capital will be safely locked into a joint future investment engine to build real, lasting freedom.

"Do not depend on others. Your own shadow leaves you when you are in darkness."

— Chanakya

"Your children are not your retirement fund. Your retirement fund is your retirement fund."

— Suze Orman

12.

"Mera Beta Hi Mera Retirement Plan Hai"

Breaking the toxic generational burden

Walk into almost any Indian household, and at some point, you will inevitably hear the ultimate emotional dialogue: "Humne toh apna pet kaat kar, apni saari zindagi ki kamai tum par laga di" (We sacrificed our own needs and invested our entire life's earnings into you). It sounds like a statement of supreme parental sacrifice, but beneath the surface, it forms the foundation of a highly toxic financial trap.

The "Shravan Kumar" Syndrome In our society, a child is often subconsciously treated as a walking-talking financial investment—a living, breathing fixed deposit or a guaranteed retirement fund. Parents happily exhaust every single rupee they earn on elite schools, expensive coaching classes, and lavish weddings, deliberately building absolutely zero savings for their own old age. While it is glorified as selfless love, it secretly creates an unsaid, immensely heavy emotional contract.

The child grows up burdened with an invisible mountain of debt and guilt, conditioned to believe that their ultimate life's purpose is to act as a pension plan for their parents. The legendary concept of the devoted "Shravan Kumar" is frequently weaponized to ensure financial compliance. Knowingly or unknowingly, parents create such impossibly harsh conditions for their own children that it often leads to horrific, dark consequences—severe clinical depression, bitter divorces, and young individuals completely breaking down under the sheer weight of generational expectations.

The Two-Way Financial Squeeze Let us observe this generational trap through the life of Vaibhav Malhotra, a 29-year-old marketing manager living in Bangalore, pulling in a handsome corporate salary. But Vaibhav is a man caught tragically between his past and his future. Throughout his childhood, Vaibhav's parents built absolutely zero retirement corpus. The very month

Vaibhav landed his first decent-paying job, his father proudly announced his retirement. Instantly, a massive ledger of liabilities was handed over to the young son—the monthly house rent back in his hometown, heavy recurring medical bills, and the complete responsibility of funding his younger sister's expensive higher education.

Recently, Vaibhav got married. Like any young couple, he and his wife dream of building their own life. They want to start a monthly SIP to secure their future child's education and aggressively save for a house down payment. However, after sending the bulk of his salary back home and managing his own basic survival in an expensive metro city, Vaibhav's disposable income is absolute zero.

Vaibhav is now brutally squeezed from both sides. Every time his wife attempts to discuss investing for their future, it escalates into a massive, relationship-damaging fight because Vaibhav simply cannot stop funding his parents. He feels deeply resentful, yet entirely trapped in a cage of guilt. This unrelenting pressure is exactly what silently kills modern marriages before they even have a chance to bloom.

But here is the ultimate tragedy of Vaibhav's life: Because he is unable to save a single rupee for his own future right now, 25 years down the line, he will have absolutely no choice but to turn to his own child and say, "Maine apna sab kuch tujh par laga diya, ab tu mujhe sambhal". The generational curse successfully completes its loop. Vaibhav's present is ruined to pay for his parents' past, and his child's future will be ruined to pay for Vaibhav's present.

How Dependency Kills Compounding Let us look at the brutal mathematics of how treating a child as a retirement plan destroys wealth for two generations simultaneously. Vaibhav's parents strictly need ₹40,000 every month for their survival and medical expenses. Vaibhav, being a dutiful son, happily transfers it. But let us evaluate this through the cold lens of opportunity cost.

The first ten years of your career are your absolute peak compounding years. If Vaibhav did not have this generational burden and had systematically invested that ₹40,000 every month into a Nifty 50 Index Fund during these crucial first ten years, that seed capital would have autonomously compounded into Crores of rupees by the time he reached his own retirement. By choosing not to be financially independent, parents do not just consume a fraction of their children's current monthly income; they completely butcher their children's long-term compounding engine. The math undeniably proves that this emotional dependency model guarantees that the entire family lineage stays permanently trapped in the middle-class survival loop, generation after generation.

Independence is the Ultimate Form of Love We desperately need to redefine duty, sacrifice, and true parental love in our society. Loving your parents does not mean you must sacrifice your financial future and destroy your own marriage. Conversely, true parental love means fiercely ensuring that you never become a financial liability to your own children. The greatest asset you can ever leave for your kids is not a piece of disputed land, a bag of physical gold, or a massive inheritance. The greatest gift is simply the news that they do not have to worry about your monthly expenses or medical bills. As a society, we need an urgent transition from the toxic mindset of "Sacrifice & Depend" to the liberating mindset of "Plan & Empower".

Summary

- **The Walking Pension:** Children are responsibilities to be nurtured, not investment portfolios to be cashed out at age 60. Emotional blackmail actively chokes wealth creation.
- **The Compound Killer:** Funding parents' basic survival during your 20s and 30s kills your most critical compounding years, ensuring you remain poor in your own old age.
- **The Generational Loop:** Breaking the cycle of financial guilt requires brutal, transparent communication and independent retirement planning.

Action Step: The Hard Talk & The Self-Care SIP

If you are a child: Sit down with your parents this weekend and perform a realistic, mathematical assessment of their medical insurance and retirement readiness. Frame this conversation not as running away from your responsibility, but as securing their health and protecting your own future family.

If you are a parent: Start a dedicated "Retirement SIP" for yourself today. Stop over-funding unnecessary luxury demands, foreign trips, or massive weddings for your kids at the direct cost of your own pension corpus. Be the ultimate hero who finally breaks the generational chain of financial dependency.

"Inflation is the worst tax on the poor and middle class, because it steals silently."

— Indian Economic Adage

"Inflation is taxation without legislation."

— Milton Friedman

13. Mehngai: The Silent Thief

Understanding the true enemy of your money

The greatest tragedy of an average middle-class earner is that they are running endlessly on an invisible treadmill. An unseen, relentless force called Mehngai (Inflation) is systematically pushing them down into the lower class. Yet, burdened by heavy EMIs and personal loans, they are desperately trying to project to society that they are entering the upper class. The brutal reality is that they are not moving up; they are simply trapped in a suffocating struggle to maintain their current financial survival.

The Middle-Class Treadmill As a society, we are terrified of stock market crashes. We panic at the thought of a bank collapsing. Yet, our absolute biggest financial enemy is sitting quietly inside our homes, completely undetected—Inflation. It is a silent thief. It never breaks into your house, it never hacks your bank account, and it never physically steals a single currency note from your wallet. Instead, it does something far more dangerous: it silently steals the purchasing power of that note, cutting its worth entirely in half while you sleep.

The "Safe" Saver's Tragedy Meet Suresh Verma. Suresh is part of the vast majority of Indians who are absolutely terrified of the stock market and strictly believe in the ultimate safety of "Cash" and traditional Savings Accounts. Suresh had no extravagant greed. He earned his monthly salary, managed his household expenses meticulously, and securely parked whatever money was left over into his bank's Savings Account (earning a meager 2.5% to 3% interest) or locked it as hard cash inside his steel Godrej wardrobe. He firmly believed that whether the global economy goes up or down, his money was 100% "safe".

With immense discipline, he saved ₹15 Lakhs for his son's higher education, an amount he knew he would need exactly ten years down the line. Ten years later, when Suresh proudly walked into the university to secure his son's admission, the ground beneath his feet shattered. The exact same course that cost ₹15 Lakhs a decade ago had now skyrocketed to ₹30 Lakhs. Suresh's physical cash was never stolen from his wardrobe, but his purchasing power had been completely wiped out. On that day, Suresh learned the hardest lesson of personal finance: playing it financially "safe" is actually the biggest risk you can ever take in your life.

The Illusion of Salary Hikes & The Rule of 72 Let us decode the brutal mathematics that destroys idle money. If we apply the famous 'Rule of 72' to inflation, and assume a highly conservative general inflation rate of 6%, the math is simple: 72 / 6 = 12. This means that every 12 years, the buying power of your idle cash is cut exactly in half. The ₹1 Lakh sitting in your locker today will hold the purchasing value of merely ₹50,000 in twelve years.

When the boss hands out a 10% annual increment at the end of the year, the middle-class employee celebrates. But the underlying math is incredibly dark: 10% Increment - 8% Real Inflation = 2% Real Growth. You did not become wealthy last year. You barely survived just enough to prevent yourself from falling into the lower-income bracket. Furthermore, real-world inflation is not a flat 6%. Today, these are the terrifying inflation numbers hitting our day-to-day lives:

- **Lifestyle Inflation (6% - 8%):** Your basic household and daily expenses are doubling every 10 to 12 years.
- **Education Inflation (12% - 14%):** School fees and higher education costs are doubling every 5 to 6 years.
- **Medical Inflation (12% - 14%):** Hospital bills and medicine costs are doubling every 5 to 6 years.

If an individual fails to strictly account for this aggressive inflation in their financial planning, their future and their retirement will be mathematically destroyed.

Cash is Trash In the old days, our elders confidently declared, "Cash is King". In today's modern economic engine, the absolute truth is: "Idle Cash is Trash". If your money is not working harder than you are, you are becoming poorer by the second. We must aggressively shift our generational mindset. We do not invest simply to become rich or buy luxury cars; we invest solely to defeat this invisible monster called inflation and to merely maintain our current standard of living.

Summary

- **The Silent Thief:** Inflation is the invisible force that pushes the middle class downwards without ever touching their bank balances.
- **The Safe Trap:** Hoarding idle cash at home or leaving it to rot in a basic savings account is a guaranteed mathematical formula for losing wealth.
- **The Real Income:** Your actual income is never what hits your bank account; your real income is whatever is left *after* inflation eats its silent share.

Action Step: The Idle Cash Sweep

Today, conduct a ruthless sweep of your bank passbooks and home lockers. If you hold cash that exceeds your basic 3-to-6-month emergency fund, that money is actively decaying. Take that extra "dead money" immediately and deploy it into productive financial vehicles (Mutual Funds, Index Funds, Debt Funds, or Bonds) where the post-tax return rate successfully beats the actual inflation rate of the country.

"If you don't build your dream, someone else will hire you to help them build theirs."

— Dhirubhai Ambani

"If you don't find a way to make money while you sleep, you will work until you die."

— Warren Buffett

14. From Earner to Owner

The final mindset shift to financial freedom

In India, we all learn how to earn money, but we never learn how to understand money. From our homes to our schools and colleges, we are rigorously taught complex algebra, but we are never taught how money actually works. We are conditioned to work tirelessly for money, but no one teaches us how to make money work for us. And because of this fundamental flaw in our education system, millions of people spend their entire lives working to the bone, yet they never achieve true financial freedom.

The Hamster Wheel vs. The Escalator The middle class is systematically trained to be the perfect "Earner". We are programmed with a single blueprint: study hard, get a high-paying job, and keep spinning endlessly on the corporate hamster wheel. But here is the ultimate trap: No matter how fast you run on a hamster wheel—no matter how many promotions you get, how high your salary hikes are, or how many overtime hours you pull—you never actually move forward. You just get exhausted. An Earner's income is permanently capped by the 24 hours in a day. To actually build generational wealth, you must step off the exhausting wheel and step onto an escalator (Asset Ownership), which consistently moves upward even when you are standing completely still.

The Tale of Two Colleagues Let us look at two colleagues reaching the end of their careers at age 55, having worked in the exact same company. Meet Mohit Rawat (The High Earner) and Rohan Shah (The Quiet Owner). Mohit was the undisputed star performer. He climbed the corporate ladder aggressively, drawing a massive salary of ₹3 Lakhs a month. He interacted with the world purely through his paycheck—buying the luxury car, a massive house on a heavy EMI, and flashing expensive watches.

Rohan, on the other hand, was a solid but average employee, making exactly two-thirds of that at ₹2 Lakhs a month. However, Rohan possessed financial understanding. He quietly lived below his means and systematically deployed 25% of his monthly income into buying productive assets—Mutual Funds, Index Funds, and commercial REITs.

At age 55, an economic downturn hits, and the company announces massive, ruthless layoffs. Mohit, despite his massive salary history, has zero productive assets. His wealth was an illusion. He panics, updates his resume overnight, and desperately begs his network for consultancy gigs because his brutal EMIs demand to be fed. Rohan accepts his termination letter with a calm smile. Over the decades, his carefully built portfolio has grown so large that it now generates more in passive dividends and compounding growth than his actual corporate salary. Mohit spent his entire life renting his time to a machine; Rohan spent his life owning the machine.

The 24-Hour Limit vs. The 24/7 Engine Let us break down the brutal mathematics of human labor versus capital. As an Earner, your income is fragile. If you fall sick, your income stops. If you sleep, your income stops. You only have a maximum of 24 hours a day to sell to an employer. But Capital does not sleep. Capital does not take sick leave, it does not ask for weekends off, and it never complains about overtime. If you invest ₹1 Lakh in an asset growing at 12% to 15%, that money is working three shifts, 365 days a year, entirely for you. The mathematical truth is that you can never become truly wealthy just by selling your own time; you must eventually buy assets that multiply your time.

From Consumer to Capitalist We must flip the script on how we interact with everyday brands and money. The middle class interacts with the world strictly as Consumers. They rush to buy the newest iPhone, shop at massive retail chains, and consume daily data on their telecom networks. The wealthy interact with the world as Owners. The mindset shift is simple but profound: Before you buy the product, buy a piece of the company. Stop solely enriching massive corporations by buying their depreciating liabilities; start owning their appreciating equity. Become a shareholder in the economy, not just a blind consumer. The ultimate truth is that financial freedom does not come from simply making money; financial freedom comes from understanding money.

Summary

- **The Medical Clearance:** This is the Book 1 of the series, which was your financial diagnosis and surgery. We have successfully eliminated your toxic financial viruses, cut out the heavy bleeding of bad debt, and destroyed the middle-class myths of show-off and emotional investing. You are now financially awake.
- **The Escalator of Wealth:** You cannot get rich by renting out your time. You must transition from being a lifelong consumer to a capitalist owner.

Action Step: From Mindset to Execution

It is time to transition from rehabilitation to bodybuilding. You now know exactly *what not to do*. You have reclaimed control of your financial life so that you never have to ask anyone, "What should I do? Will I have enough to retire? How will I manage my kids' education?"

In the next phase, you will learn exactly *what to do*. Prepare to gather your capital, open your Demat accounts, and step into Book 2 of the series. Your complete blueprint for actual, actionable financial planning and portfolio creation awaits.

Because when the mindset of India changes... only then will India truly move forward.

"Arise, awake, and stop not till the goal is reached."

— Swami Vivekananda

"Knowing is not enough; we must apply. Willing is not enough; we must do."

— Johann Wolfgang von Goethe

A Final Note of Gratitude: The Journey Ahead

Reading this book was not supposed to be easy. Over the past 14 chapters, we have confronted some of the most uncomfortable truths about money, status, and the generational burdens we carry. We have torn down the toxic illusions that society sells us and faced the harsh mathematical reality of the middle-class trap.

If you have made it to this final page, I want to deeply acknowledge your courage. It takes immense strength to look in the mirror, unlearn decades of flawed financial conditioning, and decide that the cycle of financial anxiety ends with you. You have taken the hardest, most vital step: you have chosen awareness over comfort.

But remember, understanding the trap is only the beginning. Escaping it requires consistent, lifelong action.

The Anchors Behind the Mission

This book, this framework, and the absolute clarity I operate with today did not manifest in a vacuum. I am acutely aware that whatever I am today, and wherever I stand, is solely due to the unyielding bedrock of support provided by my family.

To my parents, who sacrificed their own comfort to hand me the ultimate assets of education, discipline, and values; to my sister, who has been a constant anchor of belief through every phase of my life; and to my wife, whose unwavering patience, partnership, and silent sacrifices have allowed me to build this ecosystem without fear—thank you. You are the real, foundational engine behind this entire mission.

True financial freedom is not just about accumulating cold capital; it is about building a collective mindset. And that is a journey best taken together.

Join the Movement

I invite you to subscribe and lock your spot in our growing community of financial thinkers on my YouTube channel, **The Art of Wealth Making**.

While the platform is currently gearing up for its official video launch alongside this book series, this is exactly where the next phase of our mission will unfold. Moving forward, we will be dropping heavy masterclasses—breaking down complex financial concepts, analyzing market cycles, and building actionable blueprints for everyday professionals.

Subscribe today, turn on the notifications, and ensure you are part of the foundation circle from Day 1. Because as I always say:

When the mindset of India changes, only then will India truly move forward.

Thank you for trusting me with your time, your attention, and your financial future.

Gather your capital, protect your peace, and I will see you in Book 2 of the series.

To your absolute financial freedom,

Rehan Vijay Jain Founder, *"The Art Of Wealth Making"*

www.ingramcontent.com/pod-product-compliance
Lightning Source LLC
LaVergne TN
LVHW100323210926
848480LV00003B/1232